Chunks of Lavender

Sakshi Aswal

Writer's Pocket

First published by Writer's Pocket in 2021

email: publish@writerspocket.com

cover design by Bimal Kirti

ISBN-13: 978-93-6083-439-5

www.writerspocket.com

Dedicated to
those who wear hopes
even in the depths of uncertainties.

“Art is not one great act of creation, but many small ones. When you read one of my poems, you fail to see the weeks of careful work it took me to build it—the thinking, the scratched-out words, the pages I burned in disgust. All you see, in the end, is what I want you to see.”

- *Samantha Shannon,*
  The Priory of the Orange Tree

CONTENTS

I hope this time, you find love
in your eyes for your own self,
knowing you are a gift from heaven,
a meandering river of boundless strength.
A precious life softly rests within
the very beatings of your heart.
There are Chunks of Lavender scattered
beautifully in each corner of your soul,
just like those prayer beads
treasured by the monks.

Endless Battles

Bread and light failed to nourish me,
sleep was no longer peaceful,
even my dreams jilted me.
screaming, sobbing and cursing didn't help
in purging all my emotions.
And then, my anxious heart yelled,
"Write a book!"

- how words transformed into hope.

Neither am I afraid of thunderstorms nor of evil spirits,
untold feelings concealed within the secrecy of my heart
are quite enough to instill terror inside of me.
A peculiar feeling of being abandoned by the beloved,
or the possibility of him being snatched
by the hands of fate or God,
living without him would be like
stealing the light from days,
to be left with just cold and dark nights.
I am afraid of ugly scars
that are too stubborn and refuse to be healed,
the fear of being helpless,
to have a voice so fierce and loud
and yet incapable of being heard.
And at times, I am scared of
bizarre numbness that can evoke
beneath this delicate flesh.
What if I give up on feeling anything at all?

I can sense an unbearable ache right here in my chest,
as if an insidious arrow pierced straight through my heart.
An inexplicable pain which neither calls death
nor permits me to breathe without restlessness,
I often ponder, what if I somehow discover
a secret heaven or an entirely new land
which no man has ever walked upon.
I dream about running far, far away,
even my very own home feels unfamiliar.
Terribly tired, dejected, and full of loathing,
I walk with a cracked soul,
countless remedies failed to heal this invisible agony,
now only horrifying silences dwell within me.

- Anxiety

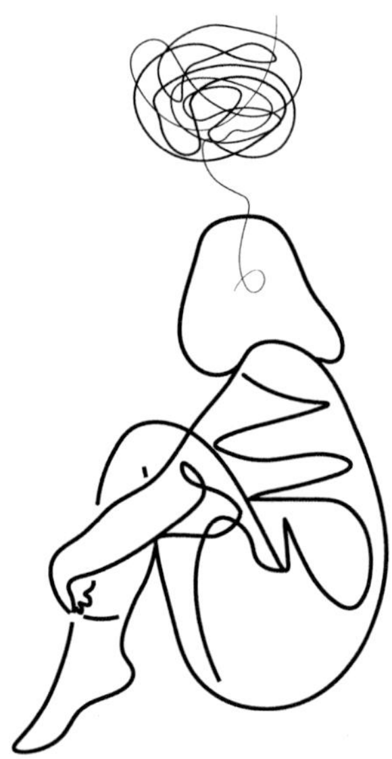

I have been holding up countless words for quite some time,
wholly consumed with nothing but just words,
some more words and a few more.
They unknowingly arise from quiet thoughts and loud silences,
fallen apricot leaves, moving clouds,
unanswered prayers and bittersweet moments.
But I tell my heart,
words can also turn into a cold companion
as some days they refuse to flow with ease.
It feels as if poetry is stuck somewhere underneath my jaw,
while other days, it is cumbersome
to carry a stream of words
that keep overflowing and do not know
when, how and why to stop.
I have quite not understood yet whether
they are healing or killing me each day.

How many of us have celebrated
the richest souls who speak of glory with pride,
those who are addicted to the taste of gold and greed
and believe in carrying the fleeting pleasures even after death.
But what about the small victories
of those who battle somewhere
in the middle of tender moments,
without craving for worldly desires,
like the monks wholly lost in their thoughts
secretly cherishing the priceless treasures,
that woman who abandoned her dreams,
worked until the cracks of sorrow were
quite visible on her flesh,
only to place milk and some bread before her child,
an unfortunate kid whose tragic eyes
stare at books with curiosity
but accepts slavery as his destiny.
Battlefields are not the only places
where you can conquer.
I have seen nodding flowers
singing hymns of praise for
all these soft unsung Warriors.

Some days it feels like the morose dusk
would fall upon me,
I stroll down the streets,
silence, starvation and grief
being my only companions.
I hunger for solace and hope
which city lights and it's hustle
terribly fails to offer.
In the midst of ordeals,
nothing nourishes my soul
except Bible and Poetry.

I could not forcibly attach
that love to my heart,
when it was too keen
on abandoning me,
for I was offering a home
that would remind him of heaven,
while the devil within him had
the habit of living in
temporary residences.

I carry no agony that
solely belongs to me.
Each one of you
have also lived with it
and this arouses both
terror and comfort
inside of me.

Ours is undoubtedly the age of deprivation,
there's enough wealth but
a scarcity of emotions within souls.
They breathe the air of trauma
but still carry false hopes.
They just know how to snatch or borrow
but seldom have anything to give in return.
Mocking others is one of the favorite pastimes
while concealing their authentic self
is the constant battle.
We belong to the age wherein
feelings are sold and little joys are dying.

It felt as if I am an unfortunate home
that has been abandoned abruptly
or the dream that remains undreamt.
Grief and remorse
followed me like Shadows.
I carried a few prayers in my heart
that remained unheard.
But somewhere, I knew
I am about to become
the most unforgettable poetry.

Like a sailor in the
middle of a vast ocean
discovers precious pearls,
I found solitude,
a strangely beautiful place
where I belong to none
but only myself.
I have tasted nothing
as peaceful as that,
but I warned myself,
it can be a nuisance too,
for the touch of humans
began disrupting me
and somewhere,
it was quite scary.

I wish I could
peel off my white flesh
until the very surface
of paler tissues
become clearly visible,
just to make them realize
that's where the real
humanness lies.

I still find a few Chunks of my soul
attached to the departed lover,
the one who gave me everything
but never his faithfulness.
I am insane in the eyes of the world,
they don't know how peaceful
it is to live in denial.
I keep searching
for those familiar eyes
that would narrate
my untold poems
just like his did
but never really found one.
Now, I am accustomed to
meeting strangers,
with the heart that still
remembers his voice,
with the same flesh
that once blushed for him,
but now seems bleak and lifeless.

My lips no longer
utter any prayer,
nothing but just
sorrow resides in
each chamber of my heart.
I yearn for a kind of love
that still believes in
love letters and soft promises.

Sensitivity clings onto me
like a moth sticks to the tree.
I hear the unsaid,
see what probably doesn’t exist,
feel for the unknown,
make up unbearable stories
in my head,
give birth to raw and intense emotions,
the slightest change in someone’s voice,
gesture or feelings devastates me.
This softness often crumbles every bit of me,
my delicate being has been
wearing tragedy for quite a long time,
and I feel remorse for the same.
But somewhere I also believe
maybe that’s what makes me a poet.

Conqueror within you

A butterfly with clipped wings
dreams of flying,
the flowers Bloom and seem joyful
as they are touched by the spring,
a woman with a barren womb
knits rotten hopes with
the sweet little warm sweaters,
beautiful memories of the departed lover
still evokes sweetness in the heart.
Leaves turn golden and fall down
to welcome the autumn.
That's how poetry beats in
all the priceless, precious things.

To all those women,
who crave to run wild and free,
in the field of light and lavenders,
I hope each particle of your soul knows
there’s a strange beauty even in between
those crushed moments,
for, that’s when you will meet
the Silent conqueror that
breathes inside of you.

My father carried poverty, hunger and decayed hope
on his shoulders for a long while,
spoke in crumbled English
and, like a vagabond, walked barefoot
in between the alleys of foreign lands
with the regional language attached to his tongue
and a little penny in his pockets,
he dreamt about a vaguely better future
wherein the world won't laugh at his inability
to utter fancy words in perfect accent,
rather his efforts and extraordinary skill will be celebrated.

When nights were cold and dreary,
his eyes yearned for sleep,
but he neglected it to feed us a handful of rice.
When days refused to be kind,
he asked the sun to bestow
a little fortune upon him.

Bit by bit, he fabricated an
entire empire for himself,
his bumpy tanned skin and earth
are the only witness to it
and yet I see his eyes flickering
with the same gentle grace.

I searched for the rarest words
and even their synonyms,
to tell the world about
how gallantly he survived,
learned and conquered.
But I realized,
he is an art that cannot be
described with mere adjectives
and the pleasantest statements.
A man who is a walking memoir
of pure resilience and strength,
I call him my father,
I call him my father.

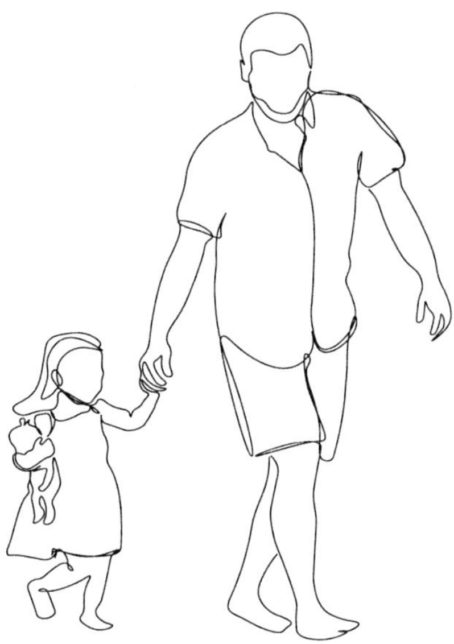

But the brutalities
did not make me harsh
rather gave me another reason
to be a little more tender
as I realized there is
a dearth of softness in
the land I walk upon.

For those born with
beautiful brown marigold skin,
you are so much more
than the melanin
produced by the stubborn organs.
Open the eyes of your soul,
oceanic beauty wraps
every inch of your being,
whose depth cannot be fathomed
by those who die for temporarily
decorated pleasant faces.

I woke up with a sweet familiar ache in my gut
as though I have given birth to another agony.
I felt a terrible urge to feast on lavender stew and poetry,
tiny little words seeped into my soul,
while thousands of muddled thoughts danced in my head,
I took refuge in coffee-stained pages
and wrote all that I could.
I do not stop binding words until it feels like an art
and my eyes look parched and tired.
Each verse silently offers me peace
as I purge all my emotions,
that were once repressed and now finally found liberation,
with pride in my heart and tears of joy,
I clap my trembling hands
and tell myself with a soft
overwhelmed voice,
"you made it."

I have misplaced my hopes somewhere
and I keep searching for them in
all the little known places.
Deep within, even I know
they have died silently.
Inhibitions and fears blended into my blood
just like milk artistically intermingles with the coffee.
Now nothing I can hear except,
mocking vexatious voices that belittle me
and have named me as a petty creature
who survives on poetry.

I begged the solace to sit with me for a while
though it will not arrive until
I prove to the humans who walk
with self-proclaimed scientific minds and empty souls
that the art which runs through my veins
will compel them to bow before me.
One day, the entire world will sing
the verses of this woman
who refused to be defeated.

The word 'Ugly' was imposed on me
while I was carrying a
half-bloomed female body,
still discovering the stubborn
and fragile parts of my very own self.
Sadly, I believed it to be true,
began perceiving even
my shadows as undesirable.
Each bitter remark remained
intact in my head,
it took me years to realize that
the freckles on my face are as artistic as
the constellations that gleam in the dark.
Beauty has no physical form,
it is deeply engrained
within each one of us,
cannot be touched, rather
it is felt, just like the warmth of the Sun.

- Changing the definition of beauty.

But I still write devoid of any dream,
the way a nightingale sings
the sweetest hymns even on gloomy days
along with uncertainties,
if the voice will be
heard, loved and admired.
I string words together
which unknowingly becomes poetry
and mends everything that lies
disintegrated beneath this wretched skin.

My dreams have collapsed a million times,
I'd swallow a few pills that
promise to grant me sleep
and doze off with a broken soul.
My weary eyes still dare to
welcome mornings with scarce hopes.
Death often smiles at me while
the demons in my head advise me to
give up on this chaotic trivial life,
but I somehow hush them
while the stars hail me as
a walking miracle.
I have made a soft vow to myself,
I will keep gentle poem alive
as long as this heart beats.

To wild women
with rebellious spirit and an unapologetic heart,
the next time, bitter sexist remarks are
thrown at your face,
remind them that,
once their delicate male body
begged for protection in a woman's womb.
A female's flesh and her organs
are the only places they have
emerged from.
Never let those misogynist minds question the worth
of the Goddess that breathes within you
You are the bearer of life and strength,
equal to all those men who claim to be superior.
Break each shell that restricts your very own being,
create history and masterpieces,
either conquer the existing world
or build a new one.
Let them name hurricanes after you,
so that our daughters
won't have to cling onto
the same terror, the same prejudices.

My partly-bloomed female body felt disgusted
at being touched by the clumsy hands of men,
I do not know whether I was twelve or thirteen,
but my flesh that deeply felt and suffered
does remember how I began feeling guilty
for carrying womb and breasts.
Even holiest water couldn’t
rid me of that stubborn dirt.
I wanted to roam around wearing
manly clothes and chop off
my long hair or everything that
echoed womanliness but then
the enraged feminine spirit within me
yelled, “they have not really
killed your grace and dreams.”
Slowly, healing reached out to me
while the world applauded for my triumphs,
my heart realized no soul can ever snatch
poetry and fierceness from me.

Blossoming
bit by bit

I was utterly weary of being
stuck somewhere amidst
the dark intense thoughts.
Bitterest wounds kept on
drowning me in
an ocean of despair,
until mushy strength
unraveled itself with grace,
and I discovered the "art of letting go."

She felt completely at ease with
every withered part of her soul,
with the flawed skin
that veiled her
and all the scars that
echoed the battles
she fought fearlessly.
That's how she healed,
that's how she blossomed.

Women have constantly
struggled to flourish.
How liberating it will be
if pride and joy will replace
envy and insecurity,
each time we see
another woman
celebrating victory.

- Applause wholeheartedly for the women around you.

Upon being asked, “what does love look like?”
I was quite at a loss for words,
how to define such a glorious feeling?
But then suddenly, my heart replied,
“as if countless purest prayers
have been answered
all at once.”
Love is found in sweet little
mellow moments,
with a gentle touch of
sacred kindness and faith.

I count a few blessings
on my fingertips,
you being the first one
among them.
You are a treasure
I want none to see,
feel and discern,
as if I've found
an exceptional love
that was buried
somewhere beneath the stars.

Let the softness
envelope itself
all around your existence,
even a bit of it
can make you someone's
"human star."

Even in the depths of misery,
whisper a sweet little
'gratitude' note
to the universe
for pouring even those
magical moments
over you which
you did not even
ask for.

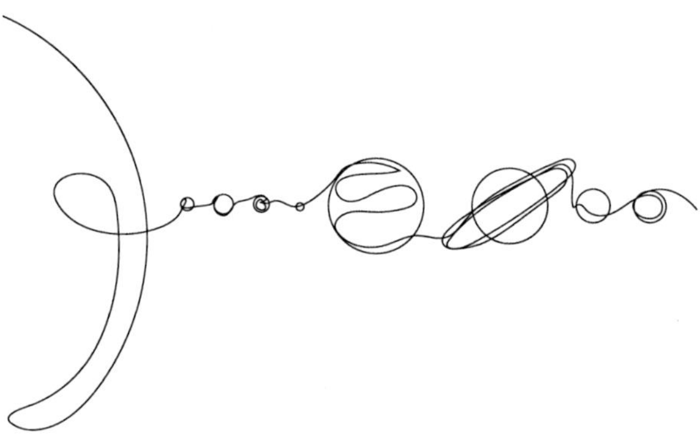

My tongue tightly holds the language of
mountains and flowers,
as sweet as the fragrance of
a newly bloomed love in the air,
though, at times, I do curse poisonous
humans in the most ugliest way.
Words and fire gave birth to me,
my lips utter only prayers and poetry.
The combination of my verses and diction
can create magic and bring you home.
There are innumerable unnamed stories
that quietly beat in my heart
and impatiently crave to be revealed.
I promise I'll gift a lot more poems
than I have borrowed from the world.

You have spent almost
a decade of your life,
searching for a kind of love
that already resides
inside of you.
Why to beg for it
at stranger's doors?
No love can ever be
as relentless as the one
beautifully curled up
in between your
fragile heartbeat.

I find lavish golden stuff
too much worthless,
nothing is more precious
to me than the purest love
spilling out of your eyes
and the gentle touch of your
fingertips running through
my lavender scented long hair.
Gift me nothing but just
fidelity and sweetest devotion
wrapped with lovely laces and poetry.

A beautifully relentless
and sacred strength
springs from your
apricot honeyed skin,
wear it with pride.

- To my brown tinted people.

I wish someone had told
my younger self that
your body deserves
so much more than the
constant pressure of
depicting itself as a perfection.
Fat, ugly, brainless, unworthy –
none of these words define you,
rather it unveils the stubborn filth
which is deeply rooted into their souls.

I am often asked
where do all these poems hail from?
How do I tell them,
I just look at my beloved
and end up sprouting
infinite feelings and honeyed words.

- He is the origin of my poems.

I felt as tired as the sunset,
tired of proving my worth,
every cell of my being gave up,
not because something defeated me,
rather, a wise thought stuffed into my head,
as I realized no one really has
the right to decide my dreams and destiny.
I am wholly aware of my soul
and what it is capable of.
My life can never be defined by
their senseless and petty opinions.

A beautiful sin quietly sits
upon your honeyed lips,
which I crave to taste.
I am not afraid of
committing this evil for you
as every bit of me wants to
melt within the warmth
that your flesh wears.
I belong to the musky fragrance
that your heart springs
and to all the kind prayers
you have ever uttered.

- I belong to you.

You remind me of –
every poem I kept searching for,
a rare magic secretly unwrapping itself,
flowers that bloom when
the entire world snuggles,
and all those breathtakingly beautiful
moments for which my heart
overwhelmingly uttered
"Amen."

To the poets about to blossom,
you can't really trust words wholly,
they are quite feathery one moment,
burdening the next.
Some days it will feel like
you are treading water
without being able to stay afloat.
Simply write every quiet story
that you have preserved as though,
they are letters for the deceitful lover.
Recite every poem that
you are too afraid to utter.

Your love compelled me
to write when I had completely
isolated myself from words.
I think I have finally found
my home somewhere amidst
the soft beatings of your heart.

- Thank you for bringing me close to the poems again.

Words are quite like
soft mercies that
muffle my whole being
and shower an armful of
hopes upon me.

Letters to the Beloved

And because I am not an extraordinary writer, I may not know the precise way to express my feelings. All I know is I just love every bit of you. The way you read all my intentions, the way your mouth curves slightly when you utter my name, and also, the way you giggle whenever I do something crazy. At times, I can be a little difficult to love, but for me, falling in love with a man like you will always be quite effortless. I just want to fill the rest of your life with love, light, bliss, hopes, dreams and magic.

With my heart in one hand and a bunch of lavenders in the other, I dedicate all these letters to you.

It's quite insane that I never really realized how rigorously every atom of my being wholly attached itself to you and when did this delicate heart of mine took a vow to pound only for you. Even though I am well versed in five languages, still in my opinion, I do not have words to describe how much you mean to me. I have spent my former days tirelessly weeping, praying and fasting. You are like one of those fictional men I read about in romantic novellas who proved me that the real love actually tastes as sweet as berries. I think if love had a face then it would probably look like yours. I have learnt to love selflessly and live carefreely solely from you. It sounds too dreamy but my poetic nerves are compelling me to confess that I swear I have seen galaxies in your eyes and the sun rising on your marigold skin. I have tasted stars on the tip of your tongue. My beloved, you are pure magic that just appears somewhat like human.

At times, I feel scared of this vague anxiousness which slowly envelopes my heart. With each passing day, my feelings for you are running wild and so is the fear of losing you. I never thought that one day a person will become "my home." Now, you are the reason for my existence. I want to mould my entire being in the exact form that you find desirable and tear apart every little thing which is distasteful to you. You came into my life unpredictably and gave love a whole new meaning. Thank you for loving me in the most raw, pure, selfless and exceptionally beautiful way. Thank you for understanding not just my words and thoughts but also the silences.

They warned me that love has a strange ability to ruin a person. I was told that love is too bitter, but then your purest devotion evoked an exceptionally priceless feeling somewhere deep down in my heart that was once hidden somewhere in the middle of honey suckles. There is nothing more tender and beautiful than this love. It doesn't make me vulnerable, rather it has become my biggest strength. I am addicted to you now and every warm touch of yours is deeply imprinted upon my soul. I have no reason to unlove you and neither do I ever want to.

Countless words are humming in my heart but still they aren't enough to describe these ineffable feelings. I love you in a way that no soul has probably ever witnessed. I do not belong to even myself anymore as you are my only origin. I hope forty years later, we will be looking at our old snapshots while smiling at how nothing has really changed.

Soft Remedies

Some days, you'll feel like miserable emotions are crawling up and hauling each memory or thought that you've been stifling for a long while. When there's a horrible inclination stuck into your heart that makes you battle even for your next breath and nothing truly mends as though somebody has cursed you with endless ache. As though million words of pain and dejection will also fail to describe how broken you are from the inside. At such times, waking up feels like the hardest part because the reality appears to be tremendously worthless. On the other hand, life tastes just like a progression of steady misery. Repeating affirmations won't actually help since somewhere, you would prefer not to feed yourself with toxic positivity.

We have consistently been educated to subdue, crush and shroud our feelings into the deepest and untouched pieces of our spirits. However, this only makes the ordeals considerably even more troubling. I can offer you simply a little soft remedy and that is – your own "tears." Cry as dreadfully as you want to because that's what offers you acceptance, without which your wounded heart can never move forward. It is an unavoidable truth that if you loved profoundly enough to be heartbroken then without a doubt, you'll have to encounter some suffering. Weeping doesn't actually imply that you are delicate or you have lost the fight, rather it basically implies you are a tender human who needs to cleanse his spirit from each agony that carries a series of misfortune with itself. You can split the ocean into two. Lift up your lavender soul and simply believe that there's nothing you cannot do.

The problem arises when your identity is enveloped by what other people think about you, your actions, dreams and beliefs. It's important to persevere your own dignity, paying little heed to others' opinions about you. There are times when people around you try to degrade you and shower you with disapprovals and it may make you feel unloved, unappreciated, and disparaged but, promise yourself that when the world starts doubting your worth, you will still never question the soul within you because you have no right to be harsh towards the life that the entire universe has beautifully moulded.

Not every person will like you or your energy and that is okay. Even if you'll gift them a huge chunk of your soul, they'll still have nothing to offer in return and that is also completely okay. Stop pouring love on those who do not deserve even a bit of it. Open your heart to those who really love you and understand that you are a soft human who is constantly forced to wear a rough flesh in order to survive in this harsh world. Keep on blossoming wherever you are planted. Stay consistent with your values and give yourself space to commit mistakes because that's how you'll learn. Always remember that there is lavender in your heart and a rare beauty scattered in every part of your soul.

Slowly and softly, you'll heal. Out of nowhere, the sun will rise and you'll blossom. Precisely when? In how many weeks or years? That, no one can really tell. But I can surely promise you that one fine day, healing will knock at your door and you won't even realize how the ache suddenly left your soul and transformed you into a much more gentle and beautiful human being. There are breathtakingly beautiful miracles hidden somewhere in the middle of little delights that the universe has gifted to each one of us like uncountable explosions of lights contrasting against the gloomy skies, the sweet scent of newly fallen raindrops and soft shoots of the plants, the sun beating down and warming your cold skin and coziest hugs from your favorite people. I hope you never forget how sad birds dare to sing even when seasons are summery and tedious. I hope you learn to embrace each chunk of lavender that breathes inside of you.

I got to know fear intimately when the pandemic brutally crippled the entire world. We witnessed a strange scenario wherein humans were forbidden to even touch one another and only despair surrounded us. A devastatingly depressive phase during which innumerable people lost their lives and science failed to discover the precise cure for this ailment as if the purest heart has cursed the world and wrenched it up. But these circumstances made me realize that all we have and all we will have at any point is this exact second and if we need to be genuinely alive, we'll have to figure out how to be present at this moment, as opposed to depending on our past or future to support our thoughts about life. This change in the outlook is truly a blessing and also the soft remedy that you probably need. For the very first time, I saw beauty in all those small mercies that seemed ordinary until now. I feel grateful for mornings, the way sun shines amidst a cluster of buildings, birds sing to awaken the sky, food that nourishes me, warmth of coffee evaporates in a mist, lavender-scented candles and most importantly, books, Bible and poetry that saved my soul.

All these poems have led me to you.

Thank you for being my softest remedy.

I hope these words somehow
planted hopes within you.

Acknowledgements

I owe everything to my father, Suresh Aswal, who is my forever ray of sunshine. His undeterred faith in me always encouraged me to work harder and achieve my dreams. I am thankful to my mother, Pushpa Aswal, for being my friend first and understanding a rebellious daughter like me. My elder sister, Dr. Shweta Aswal, who is not only an amazing doctor but also a beautiful soul. Thank you for simply being my sister and always showing me the righteous path.

Shuchi Ma'am, who has been my constant companion since I was a sensitive school kid. Thank you for being the best psychology teacher and offering me a positive outlook towards life and most importantly, understanding me when no one else did. I will forever be grateful for your guidance and kindness

My friends; Ritika, Akansha, Meenakshi, Muskan, Shefali, Ayushi, Aditi, Himani and Avya.

Thank you to the whole team of Writers Pocket and the CEO, Mr. Mohit Wadhwa, for being so supportive. I also want to thank the book reviewers and the bloggers who are insanely passionate about books.

Last but not least, a big thank you to all those phenomenal women authors who have paved the way for the budding writer within me.

About The Author

Sakshi Aswal was awarded with Vajra World Records at the age of 19 as a co-author for the anthology *Maples*. Currently, she is pursuing her degree in law and at the same time, she loves writing poetry, storylines and reading various literary genres. Her book *Chunks of Lavender* will take its readers on a journey to embrace the conqueror that resides within. Her writings have thrown light on various themes such as racism, mental health, child abuse, self care, healing and blossoming. She loves to interact with book lovers on her

Instagram Page:
instagram.com/sakshii_aswal_

Writer's Pocket

Writer's Pocket is a publication house that first started out as an Instagram page on February 15th, 2016 by 2 college students. We began with the aim of providing a platform for amateur writers and budding poets.

As a publication house, we publish new anthologies of short stories, poems and other forms of writing every month. Every piece of content in our anthologies is submitted by young writers from all over India. We are completely unbiased in the selection process and try to provide the best content to our readers.

We have also published several novels and stand-alone collections of short writings by single authors. If you want to check out any of the books published by us, you can visit www.writerspocket.com or search for us on Amazon!

Also published by Writer's Pocket

Novels

In Search Of Home *by VK Mehta and Mahek Sharma*
Autumn - The Mosaic Of All *by Roobal Gupta*
Tangled Up In You *by Tanaya Atre*
In Search Of Spring *by Shreya Shively*
The Third Eye *by Nikhil Yadav*
Umbrella In The Sun *by Harshit A. Goel*

Stand-alone books by single authors

Deccan Cliffhanger *by Dr. Ravinder Singal*
A Cluttered Mind *by Yash G. Nadge*
Neither Prose Nor Poetry *by Anuradha Bhide Phatak*
DuskyVibes *by Nikita Shah*
Chalice of Love *by Rohit K Kumar*
Naked Ordinance *by Mriga Bhasin*
Papercuts Leave Scars *by Nidhi Shah*
The God Within *by Ratika Mishra*
The Flower Princess *by Sehrish Shadab*
Fiction With A Tinge Of Reality *by Shivangi Mandhiyan*
Highly Unstable *by Mayank*
Impressions *by Dr. Nidhi Kakkar*
Meraki *by Jayamadure S.*
Nazar *by Anierroodh Raammie (Hindi)*
Seeding Thoughts *by Shivangi Thaker*
Hallucinations *by Herat Udavat (Gujarati)*
I Know I Don't Know *by Sonali Sharma*
A Wallflower *by Arjun Deshmukh*
Dusk Dreams *by Kaavya S*
From The Sunflower's Heart *by Vanalika Vaid*
Saudade - The Presence In Absence *by Rashmi Nirvikar*
The Spring Cologne *by Yashaswini Angiras*
Dhi's Oracle of Divine Epiphanies *by Saudamini Mishra*
Fitoor *by Qabeera (Hindi)*
You Are Poetry *by S.V. Aurelia*
Silent Din *by Mohammed Sami Khan*
Brokenmoon *by maré vad raven*

Ignited Inspiration *by Anjali Patel*
Her: Chronicles of an un-warrior *by Monika Bhargava*

You can check out these at www.writerspocket.com and Amazon.in!